Basic Quilting

Polly Greene

Nimbus Publishing and
The Nova Scotia Museum
Halifax, Nova Scotia
1992

92 93 94 95 96 97 98 8 7 6 5 4 3 2

Produced as part of the Nova Scotia Museum Program of the
Department of Education, Province of Nova Scotia

Minister The Hon. Guy J. Le Blanc
Deputy Minister Armand F. Pinard

Co-published by Nimbus Publishing Limited and
the Nova Scotia Museum

A product of the Nova Scotia Government Co-publishing Program

Designed by the
Nova Scotia Museum

Produced by the
Department of Government Services

Printed and bound by
McCurdy Printing and Typesetting Limited, Halifax, NS

Canadian Cataloguing in Publication Data

Greene, Polly.
Basic quilting
(Peeper)
Includes bibliographical references.
ISBN 0-919680-30-5

1. Quilting. I. Nova Scotia Museum. II. Title.
III. Series.

TT835.G74 1985   746.46   C86-080775-4

Contents

Introduction

Like other instruction books before it, this is a result of notes taken during hours of teaching the basics of designing and stitching patchwork to novice and experienced stitchers alike. I found that many of the problems were the same for people who had been sewing for years as they were for those who had never attempted to use a sewing machine — hence the title, *Basic Quilting*. It really ought to have been "basic patchwork" since learning the technique of quilting is much simpler, however large or small the project.

I have made every attempt to keep the instructions as simple as possible so they can be used by anyone, regardless of the point from which they start. I hope they are adaptable enough to be used with any pattern you want to reproduce in fabric, whether a traditional design you see in a magazine or book, or one of your own making. There are many very good books that cover all aspects of these instructions in depth, so, in addition to providing you with the "basics", I have included a list of books which deal quite thoroughly with drafting more complicated patterns and designing your own.

The most important advice I can give you is to start (and complete) a **very small** project first before attempting a queen-sized quilt. Even completing a pot holder will introduce you to all the pitfalls you might encounter. It can be done with scraps you have on hand without making a rather large investment in fabric that could turn out to be all wrong. As for buying fabric, the method that works best for me is to collect fabrics I like and then design a piece using what I already have on hand. To start at the other end — to pick out a pattern and then start searching for the fabrics you want to use in it — can be very frustrating and disappointing. The possibility of finding what you had in mind is quite remote.

Enjoy yourself. I hope this book will provide aid and incentive to the person who has long wanted to do patchwork.

Polly Greene
Sherbrooke
Nova Scotia
January, 1985

Making a Simple Template

Draw a square of the desired size on graph paper. Divide in half diagonally. Cut out **one** triangle and trace with a very sharp pencil onto a piece of stiff cardboard, plastic or other template material.

The triangle is your basic template. You might need several of them as the edges of cardboard wear down quickly. Always trace templates using the original one cut from graph paper. It is very important that these remain the same size throughout.

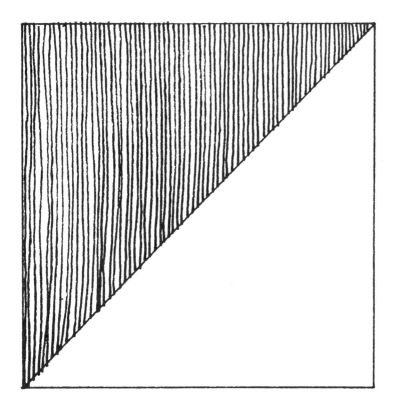

Mark each template with an identifying letter and the number of pieces of each fabric to be cut. Cut very carefully along the pencil line.

Your quilt pieces should be cut from new, good quality, firmly woven, washable cotton. Press out any wrinkles and lay your fabric **face down** on a smooth hard surface. If you use a sandpaper pattern (instead of cardboard), place your pattern rough side down (so it won't slip) on the back of your cloth with the right angle running with the threads. Trace around it carefully with a sharp, fairly soft, lead pencil. Do not use ball point or felt tipped pens. Trace as many triangles as you need **leaving at least one half inch between them.** Cut out the triangles one quarter of an inch **outside** the pencil line. You will sew directly on the pencil line and the quarter-inch is your seam allowance.

With right sides together pin dark triangles to light triangles through the pencil lines along the longest edge. Make sure pencil lines match by pushing a pin through from the front and checking the back.

Stitch firmly from one edge to the other along the pencil line. With the wrong side up, press the seam open flat.

When all your squares have been sewn and pressed lay them out on a table according to your pattern.

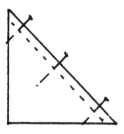 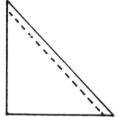 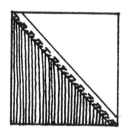

These are only a few examples of the many possible combinations of light and dark triangles. These are very old designs but equally suitable for modern or traditional quilts — the only difference being in the colors and the types of materials used. A quilt pieced in only two colors, plain fabrics, bright colors such as turquoise or pink, or large prints, would have a modern look while one done in a variety of colors in small prints and checks would have a more traditional appearance.

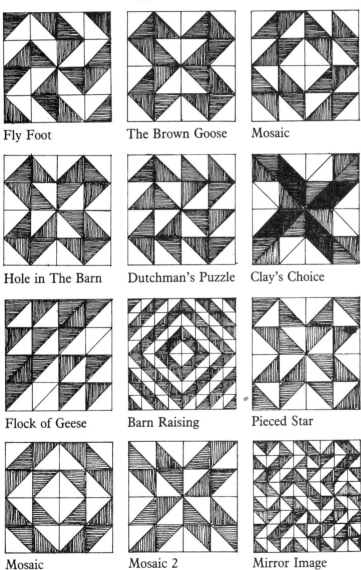

Fly Foot   The Brown Goose   Mosaic

Hole in The Barn   Dutchman's Puzzle   Clay's Choice

Flock of Geese   Barn Raising   Pieced Star

Mosaic   Mosaic 2   Mirror Image

Start assembling the squares in one corner by sewing the two top left pieces together — again with right sides together and leaving a ¼" seam allowance. Stitch from edge to edge. **Press seam open.** Sew the next two squares below these together, in the same manner. **Press.** Then sew the two rectangles together along the matching side. **Press.**

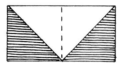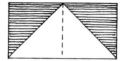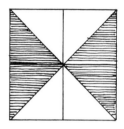

Continue assembling squares in groups of four **pressing seams open as you go.** Assemble the larger squares by groups of four in the same manner into larger sections. Keep on in this way until your top is the desired size.

Blocks may be stitched directly together or with a strip of cloth between (sashwork) or alternating with plain blocks. Generally geometrics are more interesting when sewn directly together allowing still more patterns to develop. Experiment and use whatever method you find most pleasing.

Plain blocks and sashwork can be either print or plain material but plain sections are more attractive when quilted with a design.

Fly Foot set together

or set with plain blocks

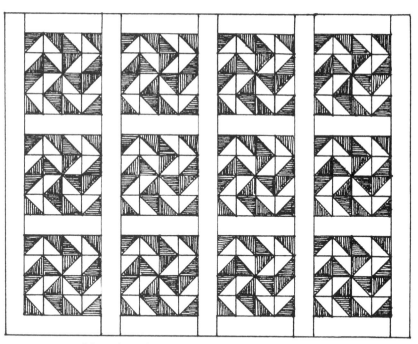

or with sashwork

Or set your blocks diagonally with staggered triangles for a "streak of lightning" effect. Experiment.

This method of piecing a quilt can, of course, apply to any shaped piece. I have used the right-angle triangle for an example because next to the square, it is the easiest to assemble and to show the many variations possible with a single shape.

Other simple shapes

Tumblers
Assemble these in strips.

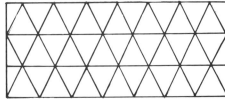

Equilateral Triangles

Combine different shapes in one square.

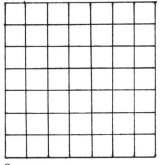

Squares

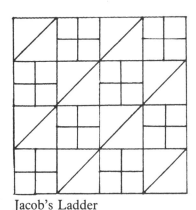

Jacob's Ladder

Squares in Squares

Storm at Sea

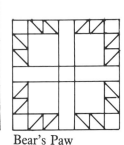

Bear's Paw

When your patchwork is the desired size, you are ready to quilt. You will need a piece for the back of the quilt the same size as your top. This can be a printed fabric (washable, of course) or a good quality unbleached or plain cotton. Lay the piece of backing **right side down** on the floor and spread your quilt bat over it. This can be of cotton or polyester, as you prefer. Piece it, if necessary, so that it covers the entire back. Now lay your pieced top over this, **right side up**, matching the edges. Starting in the center, very carefully pin the three layers together and then baste from the center out to each corner and then to the middle of each edge.

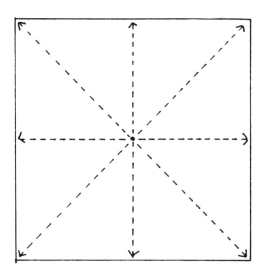

Now you are ready to quilt. Quilting can most easily be done with a large wooden hoop. Place the hoop in the center of your basted work. You will be quilting around the inside of each of your triangles (or pieces) ⅛" in from the seam through all three layers. Measure off a piece of **quilting thread** about 20" long and thread your **quilting needle. Do not make a knot.** Run your needle just under the top layer of cloth into a corner (⅛" in from the seam) and pull until the end of the thread is about to disappear. Take a small back stitch to fasten the thread and then stitch along your seam (⅛" away) with small even stitches first going down through all three layers and then pushing the needle back up through, pulling the thread taut to make your quilting puffy.

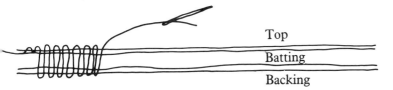

Top

Batting

Backing

When you have gone around the inside of your first triangle, fasten off your thread in the same way you started running it under the top layer before snipping it off. Cut a new piece of thread for each triangle.

When you have finished quilting to within 3″ of the edge of the quilt, remove the basting threads and trim the batting back ¼″ from the edge of the lining backing. Turn the lining up over the batting and turn the edge of the top under ¼″. Pin the top and bottom hems together.

Top

Batting

Lining

Blind stitch the two folded hems together. Then finish quilting to the edge.

A quilt made in this way will be washable by hand or machine and if hung out on a windy day, it will puff up. These directions can be used for any size quilt or for pillows or placemats.

Big Dipper or Broken Dishes Quilt

Use two contrasting prints for each block.
Vary the prints in each block for greatest effect.
Sashwork can be small dull print or a floral stripe.

Old-Fashioned Patchwork

Form blocks from two triangles of matching print with contrasting strip. Use as many different prints as possible for best effect. You can make the block any size you want. Simply draw a square of the desired size and draw two parallel lines one inch apart, equidistant from two diagonally opposite corners.

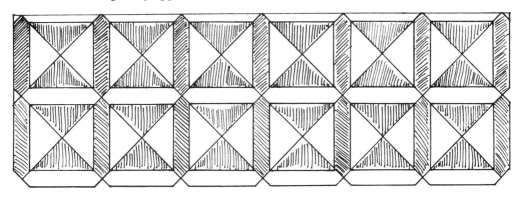

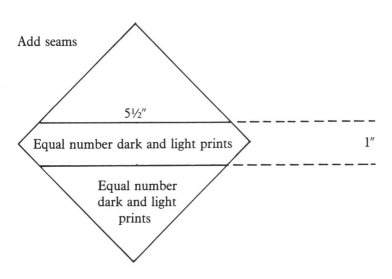

Add seams

5½"

Equal number dark and light prints

1"

Equal number dark and light prints

Squares Within Squares

The large set squares can be all the same print but the prints in the pieced blocks should vary for an old-fashioned effect.

To draw this pattern, start with the large square (any size). Find the center of each side and draw a smaller square inside the larger one. Continue in this way until you have as many squares as you want inside the large one. Each size of triangle, of course, will require a separate template.

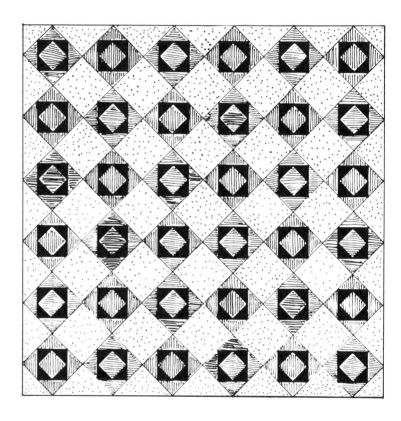

Pine Tree Quilt

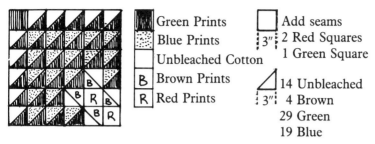

Green Prints
Blue Prints
Unbleached Cotton
B Brown Prints
R Red Prints

Add seams
3" 2 Red Squares
1 Green Square

14 Unbleached
3" 4 Brown
29 Green
19 Blue

Back with unbleached cotton or one of the prints. Add border for larger quilt.

15

Bear's Paw Quilt

Can be pieced with or without sashwork of a third print.

Each block may be pieced with a different combination of prints keeping the same over-all value.

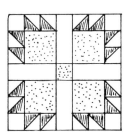

△ 16 Light Color
16 Print "B"

□ 1 Print "A"
4 Light Color

4 Light Color

4 Print "A"

Storm At Sea

To draw the Storm At Sea (16″ block), draw an eight inch square. Mark the center of each side and connect with a straight line (A). Then find the centers of the (A) lines and connect them to form another square. This is the main block of the pattern. To make the small corner block, you start with a square half the size of the main square (4″) and proceed in the same manner. The long rectangular block with the diamond in the same length as your main block and the same width as the small corner block. It is also made by connecting lines from the center of each side. This Storm At Sea block can be made any size you desire by making the center or main block exactly half the size of the complete block.

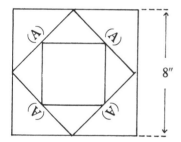

Waternish Quilt

Sew blocks into strips of desired length — Sew strips together.

3 Light Prints
3 Dark Prints
Same color
6 Background Color
or Unbleached Cotto

All one color
Medium Dark

Equilateral triangle   Add seams

Booklist

Beyer, Jinny. *Patchwork patterns.* McLean, Virginia: EPM
Publications, 1979

Beyer, Jinny. *The Quilter's album of blocks and borders.*
McLean, Virginia: EPM Publications, 1980

Bishop, Robert. *New discoveries in American quilts.*
New York: Dutton, 1975

Bishop, Robert & Elizabeth Safanda. *A Gallery of Amish
quilts: Design diversity from a plain people.* New York:
Dutton, 1976

Brightbill, Dorothy. *Quilting as a hobby.* New York: Sterling
(Crown), 1963

Burnham, Dorothy K. *Pieced quilts of Ontario.* Toronto:
Royal Ontario Museum, 1975

Carlisle, Lilian Baker. *Pieced work and applique quilts at
Shelburne Museum.* Shelburne, Vermont: Shelburne
Museum, 1957

Chatterton, Pauline. *Patchwork and applique.* New York: Dial
Press, 1977

Conroy, Mary. *300 Years of Canada's quilts.* Toronto: Griffin,
1976

Davidson, Mildred. *American quilts.* Chicago: Art Institute,
1966

Field, June. *Creative patchwork.* London: Pan Books, 1976

Finley, Ruth E. *Old patchwork quilts and the women who
made them.* Newton Centre, Massachusetts: Brandford,
1970 (originally published 1929)

Gutcheon, Beth. *The Perfect patchwork primer.* Baltimore,
Maryland: Penguin, 1973

Gutcheon, Beth & Jeffrey Gutcheon. *The Quilt design
workbook.* New York: Rawson, 1976

Gutcheon, Jeffrey. *Diamond patchwork.* New York: Alchemy,
1982

Hall, Carrie A. & Rose G. Kretsinger. *The Romance of the patchwork quilt in America.* New York: Bonanza, 1935

Heard & Pryor. *Complete guide to quilting.* (Creative Home Library) DesMoines, Iowa: Meredith Corp., 1974

Holstein, Jonathan. *The Pieced quilt; an American design tradition.* Greenwick, Connecticut: New York Graphic, 1973

Houck, Carter. *Nova Scotia patchwork patterns.* New York: Dover, 1981

Ickis, Marguerite. *The Standard book of quilt making and collecting.* New York: Dover, 1959 (originally published 1949)

James, Michael. *The Quiltmaker's handbook; a guide to design and construction.* Englewood Cliffs, New Jersey: Prentice-Hall, 1978.

James, Michael. *The Second quiltmaker's handbook; creative approaches to contemporary design.* Englewood Cliffs, New Jersey: Prentice-Hall, 1981

Lithgow, Marilyn. *Quiltmaking and quiltmakers.* New York: Funk & Wagnalls, 1974

McCall's book of quilts. New York: Simon & Schuster/McCall's, 1975

McKim, Ruby Short. *One hundred and one patchwork patterns.* New York: Dover, 1962 (originally published 1931)

Orlofsky, Patsy & Myron Orlofsky. *Quilts in America.* New York: McGraw-Hill, 1974

Osler, Dorothy. *Machine patchwork; technique and design.* London: Batsford, 1980

Pasquini, Katie. *Mandala.* Eureka, California: Sudz Publishing, 1983

Safford, Carleton L. & Robert Bishop. *America's quilts and coverlets.* New York: Dutton, 1972